T0164128

PITCH DARK ANARCHY

PITCH DARK ANARCHY

Poems

Randall Horton

TriQuarterly Books
Northwestern University Press
Evanston, Illinois

TriQuarterly Books
Northwestern University Press
www.nupress.northwestern.edu

Copyright © 2013 by Randall Horton. Published 2013 by TriQuarterly Books/Northwestern University Press. All rights reserved.

The book's epigraph is excerpted from a longer poem by Stephen Jonas titled "Exercises for Ear."

Printed in the United States of America

10 9 8 7 6 5 4 3 2 1

Library of Congress Cataloging-in-Publication Data

Horton, Randall.
    Pitch dark anarchy : poems / Randall Horton.
      p. cm.
    ISBN 978-0-8101-5227-4 (pbk. : alk. paper)
    I. Title.
    PS3608.O7727P58 2013
    811.6—dc23

                                 2012033148

♾The paper used in this publication meets the minimum requirements of the American National Standard for Information Sciences—Permanence of Paper for Printed Library Materials, ANSI Z39.48-1992.

CVIII
I have come to
chew up yr language

to make more palatable
the L & collaterals

(at the service
entrance

—STEPHEN JONAS

CONTENTS

ACKNOWLEDGMENTS

Many thanks to the National Endowment for the Arts for its generous support. I would also like to thank the Virginia Center for the Creative Arts for providing the residency where a great portion of this manuscript was shaped. Thanks to Poets & Writers for its grant support, especially Bonnie Marcus and Nicole Sealy. Gratitude to Cave Canem Massive for its "BEING" as well as my extended family, the Affrilachian Poets and my brothers from The Symphony: The House That Etheridge Built—Dwayne Betts, Marcus Jackson, and John Murillo. Leola Dublin, Melanie Henderson, and Truth Thomas, you are my rock. Thank you, Margaret Bowland, for allowing me to interpret the *Another Thorny Crown* series, and thank you Girl Model J.

Thank you to the editors of the following print and online publications in which these poems first appeared, some in different forms and under different titles:

Ariel, "Decision Time for the Would-Be Twelve Stepper," "Steal Away: An Exercise in Getting Ghost"
Caduceus, "Engine Failure"
CT Review, "Looking for a New Kind of Music"
Dark Symphony, "Dear Reader (2)"
jubilat, "Architecture"
The New Haven Review, "In the Year of Our Lord Circa 1840"
New Madrid, "The District's Park"
The November 3rd Club, "Theoretical Constructs from the South: Three Takes"
The Offending Adam, "More Clearly to See," "Thursday"
Poets and Artists, "What Lil Soul Train Did Not Know Is in a Book"
Radius, "The Power of a Literary Novel"
Sou'wester, "A Foundational Etymology," "Reified Melody in the Architecture"

Thank you Jerriod Avant, Makalani Bandale, Antoinette Brim, Ama Codjoe, Safia Jama, Tyehimba Jess, Kyla Marshell, Metta Sàma, Pierre Joris, and Lisa Thompson (Doc T) for your critique and energy. Finally, I would like to thank the editorial staff at Northwestern, with deep gratitude to Parneshia Jones for having the vision and belief in *Pitch Dark Anarchy.*

PITCH DARK ANARCHY

IN THE YEAR OF OUR LORD CIRCA 1840

The Ion *(formerly the* Amistad*) sets sail from New London, Connecticut*

a sight never to see
somebody once saw—

                          finely pilfered cargo draped
                               around melanin men crepe
                          & calico but some nude—

broken branches
                swaying
in the breeze bodies
they were—

                          how odd the daylight
                          at half-mast no valid flag flew—
                               a nation
                          above deck   pitch dark
                          anarchy fore & aft

at the riverbank's edge
                overlooking splinted reeds
wooden houses quaint—

                          seagulls frozen plumb
                          between morning fog
                               no one notices—
                          allusions thought some
                               what audacity   what
                          if—

amistad means friendship
shall we befriend another

                          human always difficult
                          to propagate as truth, as is—

it's the question curled tight
into a clenched fist

which became a why-not-
thing of intrigue   here—

                untroubled a schooner
                slicing-slicing
                      the *mist*—
                brilliant
                cane knives
                raised
                —steady now—
                      along a lag tide

—menial wakes—   almost
river bottom the keel even
& a dreg of sludge

                against dawn's still—
                      the schooner's hull
                but not forgotten

its breadth (**amistad**
not the **ion**) held chattel

                they had been men
                once before being

(re)sold (re)manacled
(re)shipped (re)landed

                (re)tried (re)imagined
                mende (said

to own man is illogical)
            what lexicon shall we
speak coherent

                of trial cadences of gavel
                sound & decisions spoke—
                      opposite a square stern

hold strong the bowsprit—

                canada geese *cry*—taken
                      without consent (erasure
                in the (re)naming

just above the esplanade)   along the shoreline
           a u.s. customs house
in the year of our lord (circa 1840—

                           today begins in earnest
                                or paradoxical)
                        out of memory's throat

angelic but devilish
      steering wind by the lee
      in the wet well
a saga—one day maybe salt cod

                              mackerel—
                          coming down (soft rain
                on the river) through the fog
                      soft rain—

Languages contain us, and we are simultaneously bearers of the codes of containment.

—Erica Hunt

DEAR READER (1)

before the cataclysmic end of the world
    whittles down to zero, before

grounding out idiot noise pushes
    in all motion skin color, before that

which cannot be defined: our terribleness
    calibrated on a triple beam scale   .or.

call it residue running to the border.
    subjective but it is about subjects

(underneath always underneath) &
    language. after the betrayal.   .or.   a thing

of intrigue: an illusion
    caught in a sound draft. the recoil

before that final echo dimming the sun
    display(ed) for the (dis)placed

more clearly to see at the end of the world.

STARING INSIDE YOUR HEAD

secretly there is a transmitted zoom
taking place, a high-tech broadcast,

little voices up in the unvirgin ear,
a world murmur, invisible dribbles

& so you have become android, almost
mechanical, a small autopilot human,

perhaps love too is automatic, but you
can't hear negation you have become

persona non grata, a joke with no punch
line, a muted five-string quartet, a deejay

spinning vinyl in the same direction,
a monotone drone. quell to the quiet,

step inside zero to hear what you can't
decipher. information based on RAM,

the megahertz alert flashing secrets,
security codes dialing you staid,

a pool of nothing, a nothing pool & *"false
faces. too much seen, which hides & keeps*

from us the intellectual state" of america
the state meant clear, so clear no one notices

what the living do, no one understands
others' complete blindness, glaucoma

in the brain. sending an SOS out there
over & out there, come in, come on in.

F:L:A:S:H:I:N:G L:I:G:H:T:S

the cry the scream   .there.   a ferris wheel
          of lights pine   the flashpoint

          bright & guttural   through the windowpane in orange
                                        more heavily than blue
kaleidoscopes of flesh
recoil against the sheetrock   stuck in the circles the girl
                            chained
to a way of looking in—   a difficult task
the field of language   to record   bodies

          being difficult   in the washing away
down by the river a door   opened but closed
of compositional diagrams   still

                                        no blueprint shapes itself
the thing everyone wants   without recourse
to be seen
                    embroidered into the ensemble
inside each eye socket   if only then a dream if
                                        hypnagogic by nature

another dream awaits if—

GIRL MODEL J

after Margaret Bowland's Another Thorny Crown *series*

(the artist)

paint punctuates her. the paint's
    drift in night's white wake chalked

alongside the zygomatic bone
    towards obliteration. one

synthetic butterfly barrette slouches
    over the left eyebrow & scores

the canvas neoteric. let her love
    a language—make her reject

the discordant repeated chord—
    perhaps inside the oil paint

but more inside love's gesticulation   .or.
    the blank gaze's soft staccato wind—

is still, if only for a moment, feral
    & the marked human frozen

grammar at the lips. classic syntax—
    in the right hand, she rubbed out

her [self], a thing of intense intrigue,
    the brush's bristles oozing pallid

matter, constructed flesh, tragic
    between what can & can't be seen.

(murakami wedding)

dubois would label your whiteface exhibit A—
   kitten i want to hug into prayer you
the budding black-eyed susan—
                 petal upon petal
but forgive me dollface you will be called
   cunt trick or maybe jigaboo,
                    a *piece* for the night.

(gray j)

a thorny crown of cotton full bloom—
    wrapped around the ovular head
                         so much history
i remember now. she could be
    a blade glittering. in the canebrake
my grandmother too powdered herself
                   —careful now—
an anglo-saxon glow
    j's eyes know not my name
                  born of red dirt.
    she could be wagadu's offering,
a *dausi* echo inside her subjugated pose
                      sliding—
in her ear *i love* a scream. quake
    my trembled body because i know
something about catgut & guttural—
                 —somebody strum
a ventricle. against which
    leaves me ledge-bound wanting
to leap—but i could—no
              & i
leap inside her gaze one last time
    to see chrysanthemums in a f:i:e:l:d h:o:l:l:a
swaying ever so gently—

(flower girl)

because she is a disastrous trope,
    the burden of being. american
                secreted
in wounds cauterized with history's salve
    she radiates erasure violets,
                the reds
drowned by white, her silk blouse
    stained to a way of being frantic,
                each long
        plait droop,
i want to learn how to paint. flesh
    a too cruel concept & nightmare
                immortal,
her hull a master-face. broken
    scallop leaves flutter—
                down
the plane of her silk blouse, sheer
    heart-exploding axils
                reincarnated
perhaps palmate. & question: why
    is albert ayler screaming silent
                in the milieu—
        crisscrossing,
a murder of crows bent starboard
    flank amazing grace, a bilateral
                symmetry
threaded through her skin. a noose
    swinging unseen in the background.

(and the cotton is high)

a contrast she will not recall the ax blade
    shoulder high.   .or.   two ravens trapped
                         perpendicular,
logjammed as beauty made spectacle
    in the odd. poststructural ideals
               dangle
cryptic her delicate neck, each gold link
    strings a modernist's view. blue butterfly
               clip
on the pigtail, something *fatale* in silence,
    in the ravens' pause. the open field is not
            open
but postured for composition as if text
    not birdbrain driven. classical dialect
            bleeds
around the elastic waist, of white & blue,
    coloring is always difficult to catch sail—
              never
at the precise moment. malice its true self
    a quotidian thing. what about the wound's
            cut
or sheer lace alongside the ruffled edges
    of her leotard. captured on oilish linen
            she
could be a girl's cautionary. imagine—
    fifty feet up looking down in the valley.

(flower girl #2)

sideways the pupil an almost klieg of light
    backdropped by an unremitting teal—
                            i say heresy
in a gridlock. theisms squat on her shoulders
    celebrating death of a flawed nirvana—: quick
                    ,then too,
she was stolen as modern art for modern art's survival,
    once a runaway
            underground—
an abstract human in the making.   of the gods,
    i think i hear that echo loudly. lampblack
                 soot feigns
rigid the tight jawline: symmetrical residue,
    history's future, in the ravine of her chin
                call it -meta-
beyond what we can't
    believe there is baptism in the body
                reckless, itself
a stratagem. she exists as if forever, as if—
    her black ice stare accidents men
                     an instructive tale—
she the darker daughter caught in morality
    almost dead, the motif even more critical.
            or a repetitive
beautiful contradiction—: chromatic glass balls
    nesting on her head celestial. other worlds—

WHAT LIL SOUL TRAIN DID NOT KNOW IS IN A BOOK

all matter boomerangs back—: color
    keeps intruding—: perhaps

it's the misgeographic rerouting
    of center—: that place you run away from

up over the sun dancing—:

material tangible—:
    & object to be & is—: mental

developing change or motor-booty-
    shake to the half note:

of what we are: spiritual movement:
    at once & everywhere—: hands

reworking constructions of the verb
    to be: from one state to another—:

yellow light before the r:e:d
    a:l:e:r:t—: wait wasn't optional

is what i told lil soul train bent
    between the lines broham couldn't read—:

he might've been practicing to sing
    all up in there like against: telos

wasn't no guns just a whistling
    tune—: a night cloud: a moon visible.

THURSDAY

waking to a vertigo [state]ment
    between calendar days   i yell

.o. suppose wednesday's imbroglio hooks
    not but for nothing else   & then

subconsciously allegorical
    one eye straggles. to the other   red i

believe hump day failed conceptually
    like monday.   & ordered promise

i have learned to be certain   is speculative.
    hypotheses no more mathematical

to cradle than lines etched in your hand.   & listen ::
    the reel/eight track or digital divide.

subtracting always already equals
    what becomes of bebop is what

i asked my-main-mane-leon. the other day
    holding up the corner—: a column liberating

his body parts. interdependent synonyms
    nothing but bone—: he said dig it 'cuz

life doesn't have to be. a recurring sequel
    the progression in the frame's [shudder]

hybrid & rainbow leon was topography
    in the air. i left my last word up.

NOTE ON A DREAM THAT IS NOT A DREAM

back of the corner diner—
a garbage truck's hydraulic deflates
    into an irregular gale, circling
counterclockwise a rabid dog.
in the gravel-filled alley
    nothing resonates with the sane
this morning. a slow-
beep signals reverse & then out
    creeps the truck. invisible
might have been the brittle man
if not for a too loud whistle.
    steam billowing under a clutter
of cirrus clouds: there were none.
anything can be imagined, why
    the girl was told by her mother
color inside the lines. beyond town
across the tracks a boy plays
    unintruded. dandelion chutes
drift illuminated
only by sight, a chagrin absent
    (((((((echoes)))))))
rippling away from roseate horizons
the red cardinal. stuck perpendicular
    over bunchgrass fading sluggish,
today's afterglow a silent etcetera—

REFLECTING ON CONSTRUCTION

walking along one lonely avenue
between me & a vigorous globe

starlight curves this gordian district.

imperfect we have come to realize
imagination breeds aesthetic

from objects caught inside a (cat-

eye) cerulean moon. immortal
shadows play amidst false truth,

lost corridors *entranceway* alleys.

along one lonely avenue walking
freedom is a concept best unsaid.

with one's self the self-encounter

in concerted conflict, an abstract
stick figure. image making it seems

& vocabularies will kill the arts.

floods of difficult angles streak
down & guttural. through the streets:

earth's beauty flowers putrefied,
cries of the dead soon we forget.

SHADOW (HINT) OF A NEW BEGINNING

almost starboard the opening
a small canyon it was spatial

though deep cathartic blue
to speak as situated within

global thawing that melted
glacier ice caps at the precipice

washing away sediment to see
the (uni)verse without restraint

incredible a throat releasing
cry not savage yet the guttural

cities' flame disintegrating into
surreal subtext greater than

upon which discovery of course
a little girl again blotted out

as if forgotten as if *thing-being*
the disintegration of our (nig)

straight through liminal yellow
alongside the lone starling

a heavy burden begins neoteric
but a deeper down in-between.

There are everywhere unheard
(as one might see deep in an electron microscope)
rigidities
      violently breaking

—Russell Atkins

ARCHITECTURE

unknowing
      we wake in refrain   each morning
      unaware   how rosewoods whisper

nor do we care in yesterday's diction
      or even give to care about

      theorems on empirical narratives
          nesting in sky——:

jackhammers tear piece by piece
      (almost brutal)

asphalt into gravel   demolition balls
      punch concrete——: cranes

pulleys & rope build more——: buildings
mark history unfulfilled
      &   tomorrow

if the sun keeps   its promise
      encompasses more of the same

      arc of motion
in a rush   to repeat   we repeat

REIFIED MELODY IN THE ARCHITECTURE

the sky will unfold in the morning,
one sparrow's zigzag interrupts light

muting its infant song. the city will
awaken to car engines, diesel brakes,

machinery filling the air, a triangle
of clatter igniting & electric. rows

of brownstones often carry vibrations,
but vibrations often refute, or maybe

narration is a lie, & perhaps wind
too doesn't hum singing like a lark.

peonies never grew here. angelo will
skip to school with opal mouth to grasp

hope but broken glass will shatter
into urine, the rank odor spoiling

utopia lost in today's good gospel.
camellias & rhodies have drooped

out of sight. wino joe remains invisible
underneath the crumbling front steps

of a vacant house. the sky will swell
into infinite sheets of cerulean, time

erased in the breeze, no one sees joe
nursing a singular flower. wild irish

rose (red wine) trickles down his throat
where flutes sing. a frail shadow puppet

railing against dawn, homeless harry
stands atop the same crumbling steps,

contemplating differences between dawn
& sunset. in his eyes time a riddle.

little marie awakens beneath pine slats,
freshly sanded floors, exposed brick,

beveled glass spreads her face sienna
receding from a dream. she will not know

change slowly blotting out the forgotten
hanging to a counterfeit rainbow. struggle

stays hidden in daytime traffic, stories
unrecognizable, time moving & etcetera . . .

STEAL AWAY: AN EXERCISE IN GETTING GHOST

subway trains careen down dark tunnels,
voltage wire splits earth's clay, sparkling

sunshine hibernates on the gothic bridge,
arches not columns but imagination's

postscript under the city's skyline, peeping.
behind each native eye collateral damage,

iron coffles deposited in memory. palatial
pristine arteries beget narcotic beget death,

the duality of life concealed. out in the open
flies circling a random bullet hole. dead body—

an arm appeared from nowhere straight bull's-
eye imprinted a visual of how life ends us

journey on earth & we ran fast without feet
touching ground almost sky-walking children

on the playground loud noises we blinked
twice to see more clearly the epicenter (we)

stole-away like spirituals in need of freedom.
foundation flinching at sound at the ready.

THE CITY FLANKED

bedazzling pitch black mayhem. & white streetlamps light
petite arteries within the margins. an absence of narration
signals frostbitten wind, coloring impure snowfalls onto
the airport's yellows & blues north bank of the river bridged
by a bridge. suburban angles narrowly define quadrants
inside our tempered ignorance. maple not murder, hibiscus
not heroin, semantic nature demands cerebral import. ears
misinterpret vocabularies fail to hear the syntax of loss
to elucidate invisibility. no bard no town crier, no postscripts
covered in wet snow tracks anywhere. this could be anywhere:
a pothole gridded & flawed you must believe in the illogical.

WHEN WINTER IS A TRANSITIONAL STATE

from iron gate to ice-covered sidewalk
it has been a difficult winter i reflect

watching from third-floor bay windows
into unforgiving nighttime you stroll

wrestle tom & dick for a dollar bill
i would give the world to you don't you believe

love is never adequate baby this city got (us)
daily struggling to survive the madness

at the edge of a crumbled cliff i stand ready
& if you gave it all up now i would leap

or say baby-girl can i be yr good thang man
for more than ten minutes i want to linger

patiently in the fm of yr snow-white static
an emergency broadcast escorting you

away if it means good-bye please don't
my red boot walker of intrigue go

understanding i sip this bourbon & lament
the body you hustle i long for myself always—

AN ACT OF VIOLENCE

there was night broken brittle
    then the flash of light. in the field

preceded by more field, cerulean
    remnants illuminated at life's

civil disobedience & anarchy—
    before morning sky unblackened

day drifted & a knife cut askance
    the air. secondary to the moan

in the stall miles away blood coagulated—
    a man called another fag but not

before inflicting death with a *flash*—
    in unknown fields, kilometers

from jagged skylines & diesel brakes
    no one heard hate echoing the knife—

below busted streetlamps hookers
    posed vogue, yet the knife

kept swinging in the air dragooned
    into the periodic prattle of leaves.

ON A RANDOM AVENUE OF PROBABILITIES

backwards there is a red finch fluttering
at an indeterminate speed rate. the city's
snowscape against earth's oblique rotation—

pedestrians do not generate footprints
nor litter. here, an erroneous spin
of the gun chamber   .or.   r:e:d:l:i:g:h:t

braving the hawk there is a streetwalker.
foolish, it would be lee morgan insane
to park bench sleep tonight. melting

slush & grunge soon will drain the too pretty
snow down street gutters. people huddle
after dark. electric lights light up

brownstones, bodegas. slender alleyways
echo nighttime again & again cold
air wheezing, frigid-hard, rustic angles

deadly street codes, undecipherable
tangibles pleading to the holy ignorant.

DOWN BY THE TRAIN TRACKS

in the rail yard boxcars remain idle.
fire reaming the drum barrel rises

steady with winter. a communal
over red-blue flames extend willingly
fingers to repeal bone cold, grappling

with lunar driven night. an artillery

of rain, the beat down kind, in haste
pelts mementos of the difficult life.
hidden in dark subtext, branches

sheltering authentic terrible saturate
a pastoral of human squalor, how

one mutt circles slow the subjugated

yelping for meat not there. they wait
stagnant like hollowed phantoms, no

future for time rots each man's brain,
a woman, too, knows trickery of soil,

footsteps evaporate each evolution
stockpiling flames to recreate ember.

secreted in the open they die soon.

DECISION TIME FOR THE WOULD-BE TWELVE STEPPER

directly above one-stop liquor store
meetings occur every hour on the hour.

across the street leaned against a church
a man contemplates which cathedral,

upstairs or down, liquor or step one?
tonight he is powerless & a scotch

offers sanctuary between sane & insane.
you have to step over used needles

full of residual blood, perhaps viral.
in the room upstairs everybody wants

serenity but secretly a dime bag & a forty.
directly above one-stop liquor store

bodies with track marks & ill livers
use monikers of forgiveness to heal

what the man across the street leaned
up against the church wrestles with,

ironic to say the least. summer
stretches long misery winter folded

into the city, tranquil air, & the moan
of traffic. he repeats to himself: *i am.*

ENTERING THE FIGURATIVE: THE OLD MAN

just at & outside the superficial of what folks seldom see
    his body construction once beautiful. now a museum

the innocent betrayal of adolescence complete. & the city too
    is it a machine the old man asked does it have teeth?

for years boulevards scuttled his frame alongside darkness

each oscillatory star a linkage to (man)made circles
    spinning obliquely the cogs & wheels

of progress.   why it swallowed whole—: him

clearly (a)typical within (re)constructed brownstones
    when the machine chews do cringe for the old man

today—: always relative to where you be at he is
    a million miles from now against evening hemline.

between night & day there is a fracture a sanctuary

slithering into the void. the old man invisible—: where
    like the protagonist from ellison's novel he could live

down in a basement's bootleg light fighting to unerase

arms legs the body. to become visible one must survive
    daily indigestions of what this model world spits out—

LULU'S ECHO

I. *There Lived a Family with a Daughter*

there is a flash flood on minnesota ave., the light
april rain thrumming against the rooftop. a bedrock

of indigo rattles inside the apartment. no one sleeps
here. small remnants left in the abandonment.

another thunderclap   .tonight.   *where lil lulu?*
a forlorn aftermath through kitchen windows will not reveal

once, the bumbling dance of mortals, the bleakness
ate itself into cracked walls, *o the despair, o the echo*

of music still here. laughter, a family once laughed
drowning, a chorus of spirituals could not save them.

there is a flash flood on minnesota ave., the light
our father's did not salvage nothing but an elegy

on the avenue, in broad day or night there is a shadow
hear lil lulu *whistling* to the johns in the alleyways.

II. DRAGGING THE TALE THROUGH ANOTHER DIMENSION

wooden clog heels ricochet faintly adjacent the difficult framework
       this dark cloudless region. bottlenecking the city's larynx
delicate oblique vowels distort too pretty a portrait
       of lingua franca. lulu wants to *la-la-la-la-la* in sporadic snow
dissipating overhead. beneath muscular nighttime
       diphthong fine one street vendor says get on down
stop & reorganize lulu.
       [state]ment: or surreal isn't tonight a figment of what
you would have been. warbling in & out green dumpsters
       beginnings are difficult tropes. we are
ever forming bodies collaged within neoteric structures
       out of pallid rubble. particulate matter. reconfigured flesh:
that once vagrant fog & slick asphalt. growing smaller—

III. *Dear Etheridge*

methodical blue-green mallards climb clandestine
over & through the point. a silver kayak slices

a chilled river, further out to the granite sculpture,
cherry blossoms have not come into bud. the hull

of the kayak scuds across aphotic water smoothly
the town sleeps tonight. angles of ocher contort

random objects, no one notices simple erasures
.or. a little boy break-dancing down by the wharf,

a pool of memory circles him spinning like bracelets,
one by one minutes drop into reverie, arriving midday

the sun is livid. dear etheridge: explain to me how
do i enjoy physical wonder between space & time?

do you know i am leftover fragments sprawled
above dark-green grass looking up at the zenith

float away? i have been reduced to sound, an unseen
motion of alphabets. poor lulu will not be crowned

the heroine, will not be rescued. a jungle out there
anxious with no eyeballs or heartbeat—now

i am sisyphus running uphill to brave the eddy
in darkness, to catch hope—: to catch light.

THE SILENCE STRONG

the man is at the border
    of the pine forest;
a little girl fascinated
    by conifers. the pollen pungent,
flowing downstream
    with creek water a buttercup petal
upside down, & i am
    more or less at the border
that man slow scanning
    muscadine at midday
between summer's equinox.
    it's a *tag-you're-it* game,
ask the sparrows piping
    between tree branches.
brighter than yesterday
    her bug-eyed pupils wonder
who am i this dark man
    all alone. she hides
now behind the lone cedar,
    of course, there is
no sound. for a moment
    we are both caught
in the black slate of noise.

SLIDING LANDSCAPE

perhaps it's the schema of place,
seeping through steel grates
    a white sluggish film
situated inside the world. see
global positioning cannot pinpoint
    ever-changing, humans
got to work it out by handshake
or ballot. landscapes adjust
    portraits, run from photographs,
the still frame disastrous. trucks creep
down streets filling potholes,
    gravel on top of gravel to build
definition: a windowless figure
can't easily (re)locate the body
    moving   always   constantly.   up
by color we pull ourselves
over the racial mountain. the rural
    decomposition of garbage,
horizontal shifts bend
lines to survey through
    degrees of changing latitude,
coordinates. we must always begin
    again this mirage, an island
in the zero void, we walk
lonely corridors resounding
    in lonely corridors, except maybe
we don't see geometries move
the same blood, vanishing
    within atmospheres breathe
jungle layer upon layer,
voices caught in a daily grind.

MORE CLEARLY TO SEE

for Ed Roberson

one could wonder simply about *nodal points*—the long black camera's
    lens, aerial shots
& each quadrangle more linear & the green ever-so-clear. rotating
    helicopter blades
churn splitting quite freely decomposition. but the brain will think not
    about narration
but it is. atmospheric within conditions weather vanes point northeast
    but more lower.
the central region crisscrossing & a shooter all focus on the [object].
    feathering away
a description of american crows murder the skyline tranquil. ignoring
    the bent trajectory
between blades the shooter looks out to get more closer in. photography
    demands sepia
through the scope but it could be a barrel. outside the grassy knoll
    certainly (shots
fired) the view under the clip of a pine banking northeast hung inside
    another horizon—

In landscape which deteriorates always to be reworked I search for the memory of a tide for a water flower for a rumor of fury . . .
                                                                    —Aimé Césaire

LOST INSIDE THE PARKWAY

And this poetry, the ever forming of bodies in language in which breath
moves, is a field of ensouling. Each line, intensely, a soul thing, a
contribution; a locality of the living.
            —Robert Duncan

running through unmarked woodland
    highlights one human silhouette
                        in motion
the creational alchemy but not so sudden
    insipid tree leaves flutter   random
                        along the path
lighted & you stumble   blinded
    by a lark   's achromatic wing repetition
        to say
you expired at half past three but still
    laddering difficult gales you sift-
                        discard
baggaged memories over a bluff
    white clouds gone too perhaps
color
never fictionalized inside yr juvenile brain
    once summer peach & hemispheres—:
hopeful   "the impulse
    quick   the force, that pushes you
to scream   to sing . . . all up in   there"
    face first through paradoxes falling & fall
sky the apathetic creek just at & beyond
                        this
artificial catacomb above ground
    mortal things surrendering to sleep
                        darkness
twists & braids the body again & again
    inside a clapboard house indigo
                        swirls—:

refrain escorts blackbirds down draft
    the washed-out vibration of yesterday
drizzling
in yr subconscious electric lights alter
    erratic discourse of movement
                         sonorously
voices grow faint until man   's image
    quite laughable now at & on the other side it
or you   "the displacement,
    allows   of a force laboring
freedom   in the secrecy of works"
it   's just the flashpoint of your beginning
    the pneumatic ecstasy of release
                        scarab eyed
human going home come home
    in the season of februaries wintering blue.

EACH MORNING A BAPTISM

that we are born & daily become dead
says something about time. it wrings

with each waning second deep love
drying up into cold sepia. we become

an ornate picture frame still waiting
for heretics to define us, however,

at day's end we sleep against aromatic
elixir of night for a chance to emerge

stumbling, screaming, stuck in a dream,
revolving to exit into tactile blackness

emerging gray, then blue waves back
at night, up towards a higher heaven

stars fall out of a lost lover's eyesight
beautifully esoteric, the process which

you believe moments can be bartered
to flagellate brain matter not the body.

BROTHERS: A SHORT WALK HOME

after Carrying the Ice for Sunday Dinner *by Eudora Welty, circa 1936*

well past the swiveled curve the dirt road continues
lined with pallid fence post.   almost
            ten years from now parchman will immortalize
these brothers' names c-o-n-v-i-c-t-e-d. walking near bolton
born to a way of seeing, they are mississippi
            barefooted when brogans should be
optional.   perhaps,
            the delta is a hot sun coruscated yellow,
there is a colorful
amber, hidden in the defiant walk the defiant ones
            always analogous to time—:
say what you will about human condition   .or.
who framed this photo black & white   who
      dictates the dictum   to which
these two will jitterbug, cut a rug almost angelic
with bathtub gin burning the gut,
but that will be another epoch—
            place your uneducated [self]
at the curve's bank & watch day   .these boys.   unfold
alongside future's promise in medias res
watch: the latch of ice become weight—:
a "never-ending." future's inescapable past.

"PICTURED" REMEMBRANCE: LIMP AT THE NECK

But blackness as an identity, assumed or imposed, is a social construct,
just as whiteness is. But blackness is the marked construct, while
whiteness is the default: it fades into a privileged invisibility.
    —Reginald Shepherd

up in the camera's blink "pictured" the wound
terrible to be-spectacle. a rough draft human grated
      echoing the dogon, given that terribleness that beauty
horror is, squeals soft—
      another zoom in & what can be seen
ideal at a moment
glittering hate as if often before
                to placate
discordant nationality. inside the throat of space-time, a recorded
squalor reminiscent of opaque infancies—
"pictured" by the river (but it could've been
               a lake) a little girl skips pebbles
  over the water's surface clearly without regard
  to the sediment each stone tokens the "pictured," how
      gravity's dead weight drags
certain refusals of the body with (us)—
our skeleton tendered by the heart. but still—

running inside the eyes of the world a witness, "pictured"
hanging right-side up from a cedar. the construct
      inverts the default do hum *amazing grace*—
which too is a field within its-self.

MORNING MATTERS

but before i could awaken the gawd-awful scream
outside—skeletal branches, bent by the breeze, mapped
into a cold new awakening my eyes wanted to open—   (I)
      come from many different subsets, & yet
         believe this fascination with the body,
line level to a misunderstanding, plumb
terrible. the man below my audio at the top of his lungs—:
      what i heard true to form that we exist
only in mind & so the second gunshot.
spinning,
      spokes of a bicycle wheel, silent
silver reflections down dirt roads against light
screaming. modernism failed. for real
      somebody died.
upstairs, i awoke at parade's rest,   (again the scream)
a new direction i wanted to go
retrieve the bicycle,   stop the spinning,
bang is forever,   outside my window,
leaves rustling in the wind swirl.

ANARCHY

even the dark sounded devoid
of ideas, there were none as gray

began to emerge but not before
raindrops from above. walking

underneath night's allegory
on the brink of ruin i inhale

winter. & strange birds tweeting
in a tree shaded by invisible

electrons, a flesh & blood world
eats its young: a horrible joke

from this awakening moment
atavistically—: back into silence

each night brings me one closer
to the hereafter, more or less

i stand idle like a mannequin
stuck inside a window front,

the reflection projected still
puzzling: skin dilemma hung.

DOWN DEEP IN THE CAVITY

i have never been dumbfounded by tremolo singing birds,
the sound so natural against rustic woodland air. baraka

asked *how you sound,* meaning our vibration ain't quite
right. too much tremble in the tenor that we transport

evolution steeped in hyperbole, a bag of insignificant wind
we deny something human in aesthetics: the human pulse

weakened: each attempt at sound imitates a war, a friction
against that which opposes how we reside in circles, & fail

because we reside in circles. perhaps we need group history,
or perhaps we need a group hug to catch up posthaste

with the past. an unknown future inside a choir box once
we sang of promise, the trauma everlasting i want to lean into

misunderstandings tone-deaf & brain-dead, how we hear
vocal cords' resonant memory. under the ocean's waistline—

THE POWER OF A LITERARY NOVEL

in the abandoned clapboard on the second floor
on top of an antique curio a book's spine

open to the scene in *beloved* where sethe
lawd she done killed her baby. notwithstanding,

the book needs to begin again the narrative.
nobody wakes up or sleeps here, like what

changed the course of a family evicted
thrown onto sidewalk pavement. not permitted

to catch western civilization's callous spirit
a girl's throat displays a purple necklace

of perforated skin. all alone upright she sits
in the abandoned building on the second floor

her lips still want to know why. in the closet
a body decays simultaneously with summer.

she dead too like sethe her mother could not
watch a tragic slave so she slit her voice.

the prescription unattainable the pain intense,
an orange-red robin outside on a tree branch

looking through the windowsill will never know
dearly beloved or the dead baby rotting silently.

WAIL THE SINNER

after William H. Johnson's Going to Church, *circa 1940*

not even two hours
    out the juke joint
bourbon breathed
       lil jimmy
up from the choir box arose
sangin' "precious
       lawd"
still he reeked the first note
sister maybel cried   her fan
      swung
side to side to the wail & moan
  mirroring the preacher's
scream   reproduced bluemythographies
      of sweat
but creation's arms
       extended
back further up through
lil jimmy's rendition—
     of *going to church*
he migrated
momentarily   south-
     westward
the pines faced the blue wood house
yards from an oxcart
     rolling
down clay dirt road
     to the congregation
simply   naive
jimmy's solo   a call
     few could hear
even when he shouted.

A FOUNDATIONAL ETYMOLOGY

we could call it the new south or the old jook:
music manifested as condition, call it social
dog bites & dynamite detonation in the yesterday—

placards cascading down eighth avenue held
high with black letters a city spouting anger.
mute the voice nobody heard *please* or *may i*—

perhaps *fuck you* is the only way to really hear.
we could call it ill repute or r:e:d:l:i:g:h:t
splattering the floor gin lipping a mason jar.

call it fragrant honeysuckle & muscadine—
throughout the bootleg house pitch dark anarchy,
call it drunk or feeling no pain as in guttural—

call it shovel or spade & dig down to the root.
call it mojo or a callous man can make a woman
moan into the sun over the blues—*honey*.

UNDERNEATH A CEILING OF HISTORY

on the horizon the dark pitchsong
from which life springs. a womb
    at night vagabond planets align
the skyline stagnant like i remember

midnight & the eagle owl questioning
why we walked over broken twigs.
    little boy eyes we had shone a dream
faded into another dream—

the bedlam of time often an enemy,
my description:

> *we often forget*
> *what we need to remember*
> *we forget*

not far from home decades ago
time stood idle   .or.

more specific boundaries
corral, in most cities, people & conquer
    identity by color. we played with our own
day after day. vulcan, the god of metal,
watched over us denizens or so they said—

no one thought ogun in the equation.
    not greek but iron-ore themed,
our magic city—

coming to grips with the monochromatic,
i never did *feel like a motherless child.*

so much past wrapped in an unknown future
    still, i am black & cherokee, & red clay
        dna from blood
the way human emerges despite fragments.

STIRRINGS IN THE NIGHT

there are pine trees sticking out
    the side of a mountain. an incline

to hike a ragged path laid by foot-
    prints pressed deep into broken

twigs covered by unsullied snow
    at midnight. a half-moon radiates

beauty dead in its tracks: a buck
    idle as petrified oak at the faint

noise lingering. beside a runaway
    critter perhaps a wolf balanced

in the horizon. a star's rim above
    darkness quickly heading north—

swift breath & no one is alone
    on the fringe. wide awake an owl

far from urban jungle of glitter
    between outstretched leaves. yellow

light billowing irreversible silence—
    through each branch a road map

diagramming: a chinook, a whoosh—

ENGINE FAILURE

we posit
    finch & think sparrow

angling. the hypotenuse
    of sun

adjacent to butterflies
    across wretched sky.

a raccoon's image
    through the screen door

music bellowed out
    eager. children

up & up between rope
    they jump. high

over cumulous clouds
    a jet screeches

loud. into the evening
    engine failure

tailing out the sky
    a clothesline, dangling

haphazardly. wind
    breeches the border

of shadowing. smoke
    flame dead the jet elided—

FLIGHT PATTERN & HOLDING SINCE BEFORE

unlike eastern regions the dim skyline reigns
above scatter clouds, a pale shriek of lights

seemingly at parade's rest besiege the city,
blackness in full bloom stares back upward

at the plane, gravity triumphs sooner than later.
passengers will exit out into tactile dark,

antebellum architecture offering the duality
of haves & have-nots: neon ash rinses

magic this place with its iron-ore deposits.
there will be guardrails along interstate 20

to guide unlike before those terrible years.
transitioning is always complex, to switch

lanes: objects appear distorted in glass
caution: *we often see signs & miss signifying*

even the atmosphere when the skyline is dim.
drawn deep in red dirt boundaries just below

the chaotic surface. old south on the horizon
no one seems to remember. that faint echo—

[IV]

It's the ongoing repression of the primal scene of subjection that one wants to guard against and linger in.

—Fred Moten

HOME SWEET HOME

say then red clay marks the proverbial x,
a familial nexus to where i migrate.
    soil of my grandfather's father, dirt
roads fragrant with muscadine,
a small token & broken dialect sweet
    upon tongue languaging the brain.
youthful eagerness to adore somehow
this pine ridden place with iago sparrows
    purposeful in trajectory, aesthetic value
raped through whiteout, a sun not
brighter than x welded in remembrance—
    juke joints more alive with rhythm
climbing palisades. as a child i knew
nature, metaphor & the mercurial.
    call it then a falling meteor at night,
hazily the sky polluted by ignorance,
southernism's brilliant staccato
    to remind location never washes away.
& over hillside acreage hues of ocher
i can see clear between northern cities.
    the mind a trickster god completely
clothed, something odd perhaps eshu,
leaning on cane to rearrange the beauty
    of fireflies in mason jars at midnight.

DEMARCATIONS

perhaps in a city looped by train track
of iron. perhaps rabbit ears peaking up

inside the hat three-card monte. center
stage a tangible body broken eons ago

before the link between real & unreal,
to believe shadows can (re)exist under

so much weight but humans have known
less. the wooden nickel behind the lobe—

52 playing cards only one can be pulled
miraculously in & of itself, the metaphor

basking oftentimes brilliant, as if by magic
a collective resistant & we should resist

the loop a cycle to locate trauma inside
laughter amazingly. digital lights light

arteries within a city much rural darkness
just outside edges secreted is the secret.

directly parallel to winding railroad track
at & on the other side, synthetic blues.

gray shotgun shacks reside on the border
& further back perhaps the back of a bus

people had to deal with a lineage of race
at the cross. before guardrails laid down

there was always a sense of r:e:d a:l:e:r:t.
safety in volatile numbers abundant,

or skin became comfort became a pride:
we not wild animals someone screamed,

on the six o'clock news a troubling nation.
idle days the rainbow stretches too wide

against difficult zephyrs before the tornado.
listening at the intersection of vernacular,

between two office buildings downtown,
north of the lone greyhound bus station,

aging department stores lace one skyline.
the other unraveling complicated symbols

to understand anger tuned critical, lost
in translation, chaotic memories of hate.

BROTHER KEEPER WE GONE LEAP INTO A BRAND-NEW THANG

the window*pain* is a gateway to hurt
rolling down the hill*s*/ide. we navigate

landscape altered & forever twisted
in the cane break, or cain broke repeatedly

his crooked oath. our downpressor
brother artist ceaselessly has tried to blot out

darkn(us) with a misremembered horizon
almost drowning. a diminutive tear

barely noticeable but nonetheless.
no shelter for the eternal fugitive who

wanting to fly away through the pane
flies——: at a moment's notice, sneaks

through the square structure so bent
on x-ing (us)——: a storied beauty.

CULTURAL CENTER ON THE RIVERFRONT

the painting being dissected in the art gallery
inquisitively by onlookers behind tasseled rope

is forever misunderstood, a predictable outcome.
the painting (itself) on wooden easel knows that

green overlooking blue is not willow over river
but inauguration of human, & wind wanders

careful at the precipice of intelligence. black
dots are not birds, only shuddering reflections

of a noontime sun not there, but behind there,
wherever there is no one knows, for certain

the painting thinks its rare label is more than
priceless. it is a joke on people contemplating

sensory & complexity only in the natural world,
disastrous as it seems this becomes misnomer

to the crowd standing behind the rope looking
silly. real value lies behind each brushstroke.

BIRD & DANDELION: AT THE INTERSECTION OF ERASURE

pulling its hollowed bone over broken acreage
      the bird vacates quick into a break
note: outline fluttering the lake's crippled wake
& gone now. the raven sings once
      before bird it could've been. perhaps human
             in a holding pattern
     i am more intrigued by the outline. gone
          rising above the lake ruderal
          colonization, as before (us)—
          but bright terror
in the blizzard—again. it's snow"""g an open field
     against the [state]ment. but also the raven
          a priori *in the beginning*
the grenadine sun. tarantella
    shudder call it new eden, stolen
          residue. spate draft
caravan of looping wildlife
    images (re)imagined outside the radius.

THE DISTRICT'S PARK

against the grain her arm
   interlaces around mine softly
                  i feel
oppositional the current thick her blood
   a future blueprint of children
           we have
none   so eclectic the goldenrod sky
   littered with mallards quivering
two clicks starboard
                      the wind
swirls   backlash in ripples
   the lake's fabric holds (us)
                   be-
tween night & day is it love
   i ask to not know   how
               high
a function of time am i sprung
into her magic   i need to
              swan dive
fade away   *honey* she jazzes
as if music interrupted
   behind her milk crates i go
            natal
right then infected my hips
motionless the body still
            listening
for breakdown—: i jump in the riddle
        to solve her   paradox
constantly shifting   my nose
   an illusion i smell   wide open.

WOODLAWN

the road circles the river by the dock
a pontoon moored to cleat—: geese

traveling downwind alongside gravity
around the lake kids bicycle—: spokes

reflecting noontime & a couple walks
out to unleash twine made of hemp

& surface over the dark-blue autumn
months away but now summer—: hangs

lazily leaving the dock against wind-
spray a current untangling itself under

schools of carp angled upward the sun
& water does open one's sense—: of self

the couple lives singular but atypical
fundamentally as the thing essential—: god

but let it be love & not the backhand
slap the sun a kaleidoscope a gold—:

THE LAKE'S REFLECTION

unlike venice this isn't a water city, aesthetic
lakes accent woodlands too thick to diagram.

skyline opens a tedious gray, dragonflies break
swiftly over the water's surface. one solemn face

looking into a woman's reflection. sometimes
bodies transparent themselves. the woman

graven but more by gravity's deadweight. down
& through ravines a lone eagle sings. graffiti

scribbled on the moving train out of focus,
the woman blinks twice to see herself clearer.

by the prosthetic arm attached below elbow
her "hand" grazes over an outline to brush away

wind blowing her hair into sight, irises burned
by the sun (hung) in the horizon before noon.

TIME MOVING & ETCETERA——: A BLOCK TALE

at the end of the block a bucket. one boy bangs,
    almost bankrupt & sliding, the sun slips a notch
as if (re)telling a parable: *we keep on the repeat*

what echoes the repeat. multispectral
    sunlight off the wooden telephone pole breaks
splitting coolly in half the clapboard five & dime

colligated with k's nail salon. crooked shadows
    amplified along the sidewalk's rugged surface
dance: each outline engaged within itself a jig

controlled by restated bangs. the banging boy
    on five-gallon bucket hidden but then too, loud.
at half past one pedestrians animate the block

& the boy's upturned baseball cap collects copper
    sometimes silver, proving morality does exist
if for a second. summer's skin altering heat

a nonfactor to the amen corner seated under
    the maple, each man's pupils petrified. knotholes
stoop sitting minus the stoop at ground level

they memorized jackie robinson by the radio
    eternal. in the middle of (a)historical erasure
& passing by, the narcoleptic hooker from seoul

advertises *me love you long time.* seductively,
    zombie walking with a holocaust of brain cells
drowned in odorless narcotic, she longs to be

cuddled by love's brutal beauty camouflaged
    in the pistol's cocked trigger. a little girl
lodged inside a fifth-floor apartment coloring

on white paper, crayon skies, wondering—: but
    more with imagination, (re)imagining a world
unlike outside the fifth-floor windowpane

down below. underneath the whole block lives
    as under, as in—: the thing essential within human
memory. many will (mis)remember the *bang*

on five-gallon bucket. the boy at the corner banging
    into a novel morning. what vanishes will become
(mis)repeated, (mis)read. foundation, the echo—:

THEORETICAL CONSTRUCTS FROM THE SOUTH: THREE TAKES

x. "something in the milk ain't clean"

in cases of cultural strangulation (it stands out
    through projections of objects) elvis presley knew

but refused to disclose the idea behind blue suede, why
    them shoes disregarded a tradition, even the hips

didn't swang, naturally, my uncle bud had once said
    something in the milk ain't clean. with how he move,

hell that ain't nothing but little richard bleached!

y. "ain't nobody mad but the folks that don't get none"

the first trouble sign is french vanilla coffee,
    not that we need fanon to tell us, (us) the proletariat

understand when little ankle-biting shih tzus appear,
    suddenly owners want to revitalize, reconstruct,

having mad-dashed earlier for green scenery.
    it would be arrogant to think we mad, 'cuz we ain't;

however, that don't mean we ain't gettin' wretched.

z. "hanging out like wet clothes"

the women switched hip & the block-boys failed to whistle
    even though they were hanging out practicing art,

instead of *ooh-wee baby you is fynah than government cheese*
   they smiled & resumed signifyin(g), inherently

not learned in third period english literature, not from gates
   but bo-willie & paperboy said *you gotta make language cut.*

across the street i could hear somebody's momma 'bout to get it.

LOOKING FOR A NEW KIND OF MUSIC

There is never any end. There are always new sounds to imagine; new feelings to get at. And always, there is the need to keep purifying these feelings and sounds so that we can really see what we've discovered in its pure state. So that we can see more and more clearly what we are.
—John Coltrane

woman in the park ponders. guitar strapped
   across her shoulder—: elbows bent

momentarily :: multiple hypotheses ::
   running inside the skull :: structure ::

·chordal notes concealed :: how many
   remembrances must form :: refrain ::

epigraphs appear—: slowly
   possible sets of solutions to a musical

  to be born or reborn .here.
     inspiration :: a lineage of field hands—:

four-part melody :: sound taking shape::
       :: pick up

—: pick the feet up then faster
   retrograding the woman runs—: to advance

thumb strokes can be transcendental,
   a new dialectical is what she after.

SCREAM'S ECHO

a broken dandelion dangling upside down its neck
       snapped by autumn & wind's wrath
regarding weeds. lazily through the field
just before the moon's rim,
       june bugs circle themselves. the melanin green
but darker over earth is nothing but a zip
in—   time & out—
       a sapling bone splinted,
up above one lone pine a hawk hangs
superseded as omnipotent.
            all sound
marked hieroglyphics as if telescopic retrieval
       of a memory forgotten. oblique & bent
the event sequestered until now:
harking antiphonal a church choir-
       box solo. in scream's extended voice
the extractional shudder laryngitic but still
sound echoed from the refusal to continuum
  or emphatic catalogue
  —a quasi crackle. dramatic release
as if the field we were in pulled us out
to a new in—
         on the other side of that
near aesthetic lakes—flashing
"perhaps seen"
       at half intervals
trees too were a thing of intrigue against which
the blink of lights jettison
a new dawn shimmering the leaves.

POSTRACIAL POSTSCRIPT

----

upward one finger snarled toward heaven attached
to a woman

iphones would've captured much more the vibration
of those gone

ask her about decades past & billy-club nightsticks
she will say:

in the new south renaming never properly vanishes
the body

from double history: the whiteout vision of selective
& unequal—

but we move on she will inform you before asking
for change.

----

among lazy walking pedestrians an unspent sun sits
stunningly idle—

fresh mowed bermuda scents the neighborhoods
unapologetic which

stayed the course reworking jangling discourses: say
it loud—

filled sanctuaries & one sunday morning damn early
death came—

say the universality we seek lingers in the differences
we are.

DEAR READER (2)

I/must be given words to refashion futures/like a healer's hand
—*Kamau Brathwaite*

whatever thoughts i transcribe   know
   behind each traceable pattern
                is a veil
of armor   a mask to shield
   imperfect impurities judging
              me
while i judge   .you.   really
   eliminate learned language
              i would love to
reach back to primordial grunts—:
   the mere infancy of speech
              killing
the sun into black i am an advocate of
   back to universal darkness
before color diluted man's brain
              how
about neoteric images to dispel
   what is & ain't   we need a new (us)
              without
sign & signifiers of red memories
   i want to reverse to erosion
              hate
back into unbridled love   dissolve
   the corporeal unmapped & possible
              let's
in each epoch suspend the scream—:
   invent accurate yardsticks
              to study
.the unmentioned.   .the unnamed.
   mistakes not to create by evolution.

NOTES

The critical and creative texts that led me to *Pitch Dark Anarchy* are too numerous to name; however, I would like to make mention of certain works that I found useful: Maurice Blanchot's *The Station Hill Blanchot Reader,* Jacques Derrida's *Margins of Philosophy,* W. E. B. Du Bois's *Souls of Black Folk,* Robert Duncan's *Bending the Bow,* Erica Hunt's "Notes for an Oppositional Poetics," Pierre Joris's *A Nomad Poetics,* Andrew Joron's *The Cry at Zero,* Nathaniel Mackey's *Discrepant Engagement: Dissonance, Cross-Culturality, and Experimental Writing,* Toni Morrison's *Playing in the Dark: Whiteness and the Literary Imagination,* Fred Moten's *In the Break: The Aesthetics of the Black Radical Tradition,* Aldon Neilsen's *Black Chant* and *Integral Music: Languages of African American Innovation,* Friedrich Nietzsche's *On the Genealogy of Morals,* and Charles Olson's "Projective Verse."

Page 10: Quote taken from Charles Olson, *Human Universe and Other Essays* (New York: Grove Press, 1967), 5.

Page 13: The poem "Girl Model J" is an ekphrastic interpretation of the *Another Thorny Crown* series by Margaret Bowland.

Page 15: In the section "gray j" of "Girl Model J" *wagadu* refers to the tale of Gassire's Lute, which is taken from an ancient epic known as the *Dausi.*

Pages 47–48: The first quote is taken from Amiri Baraka's "The Changing Same (R&B and New Black Music)," in *The LeRoi Jones/ Amiri Baraka Reader,* ed. William J. Harris (New York: Thunder's Mouth Press, 2000), 187. The second quote in the poem is taken from Maurice Blanchot's "Literature and the Right to Death," in *The Station Hill Blanchot Reader,* trans. Lydia Davis, Paul Auster, and Robert Lamberton (Barrytown, N.Y.: Station Hill, 1999), 360.